© 1992 United Feature Syndicate, Inc.

© 1992 United Feature Syndicate, Inc.

© 1992 United Feature Syndicate, Inc.

© 1992 United Feature Syndicate, Inc.

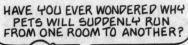

HAVE YOU EVER WONDERED WHY PETS WILL SUDDENLY RUN FROM ONE ROOM TO ANOTHER?

© 1992 United Feature Syndicate, Inc.

THAT OUGHT TO KEEP HIM WONDERING

9-14

JIM DAVIS

© 1992 United Feature Syndicate, Inc.

© 1992 United Feature Syndicate, Inc.

© 1992 United Feature Syndicate, Inc.

© 1992 United Feature Syndicate, Inc.

CHEER UP, GARFIELD! LET A SMILE BE YOUR UMBRELLA!

THAT'S WHAT MY AUNT EDNA USED TO SAY

TILL A BOLT OF LIGHTNING BLEW HER DENTURES CLEAN THROUGH THE GARAGE DOOR

JIM DAVIS 10-8

© 1992 United Feature Syndicate, Inc.

PLAYING HIDE-AND-SEEK WITH ODIE IS NO BIG CHALLENGE

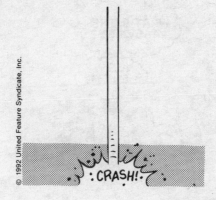

© 1992 United Feature Syndicate, Inc.

I'M SORRY. WERE YOU USING THAT CHAIR?

THIS LOOKS LIKE A GOOD PLACE TO MAKE CAMP

© 1992 United Feature Syndicate, Inc.

MUNCH
MUNCH
MUNCH
MUNCH

JIM DAVIS 10-21

© 1992 United Feature Syndicate, Inc.

© 1992 United Feature Syndicate, Inc.

HE SEEMS ALMOST LIFELIKE

I HATE YOU

JIM DAVIS 11-3

© 1992 United Feature Syndicate, Inc.

© 1992 United Feature Syndicate, Inc.

JIM DAVIS 11-13

© 1992 United Feature Syndicate, Inc.

fluff
fluff
fluff

fluff
fluff
fluff
fluff
fluff
fluff
fluff

JIM DAViS 11-20

JIM DAVIS 11-21

© 1992 United Feature Syndicate, Inc.

© 1992 United Feature Syndicate, Inc.

© 1992 United Feature Syndicate, Inc.

I **TOLD** YOU NOT TO EAT YOUR ICE CREAM ALL IN ONE BITE

JIM DAVIS 11-30

JIM DAVIS 12-2

© 1992 United Feature Syndicate, Inc.

JIM DAVIS 12-5

© 1992 United Feature Syndicate, Inc.

JIM DAVIS 12-8

© 1992 United Feature Syndicate, Inc.

© 1992 United Feature Syndicate, Inc.

CHRISTMAS IS COMING

JIM DAVIS 12-14

© 1992 United Feature Syndicate, Inc.

© 1992 United Feature Syndicate, Inc.

© 1992 United Feature Syndicate, Inc.

OTHER GARFIELD BOOKS IN THIS SERIES

COLOUR TV SPECIALS

Here Comes Garfield	£2.95
Garfield On The Town	£2.95
Garfield In The Rough	£2.95
Garfield In Disguise	£2.95
Garfield In Paradise	£2.95
Garfield Goes To Hollywood	£2.95
A Garfield Christmas	£2.95
Garfield's Thanksgiving	£2.95
Garfield's Feline Fantasies	£2.95
Garfield Gets A Life	£2.95

GARFIELD COMIC ALBUMS

No. 1 Sitting Pretty	£2.99
No. 2 Words Of Wisdom	£2.99

All Ravette Books are available at your local bookshop or from the address below. Just tick the titles required and send the form with your remittance to:-

B.B.C.S., P.O. BOX 941, HULL, NORTH HUMBERSIDE, HU1 3YQ.
24 Hour Telephone Credit Card Line 01482 224626
Prices and availability are subject to change without notice.

Please enclose a cheque or postal order made payable to B.B.C.S. to the value of the cover price of the book and allow the following for postage and packing.

U.K. & B.F.P.O: £1.00 for the first book and 50p for each additional book to a maximum of £3.50.

Overseas &   £2.00 for the first book, £1.00 for the second and 50p
Eire: for each additional book.

BLOCK CAPITALS PLEASE

Name...

Address...

....

....

Cards accepted: Mastercard and Visa

Expiry Date........................... Signature...